SACRAMENTO PUBLIC LIBRARY

D0194601

CENTRAL LIBRARY
828 "I" STREET
SACRAMENTO, CA 95814
JAN - - 2003

WITHDRAWN FROM COLLECTION OF
SACRAMENTO PUBLIC LIBRARY

Written by Betsy Franco
Illustrated by Stacey Lamb

Children's Press®
A Division of Scholastic Inc.
New York • Toronto • London • Auckland • Sydney
Mexico City • New Delhi • Hong Kong
Danbury, Connecticut

For James
—B.F.

For Charles Schulz
—S.L.

Reading Consultants

Linda Cornwell
Literacy Specialist

Katharine A. Kane
Education Consultant
(Retired, San Diego County Office of Education and San Diego State University)

Library of Congress Cataloging-in-Publication Data
Franco, Betsy.
   Silly Sally / written by Betsy Franco ; illustrated by Stacey Lamb.
      p. cm.—(Rookie reader)
   Summary: A little boy finds different ways to make his baby
sister smile.
   ISBN 0-516-22492-1 (lib. bdg.)   0-516-27343-4 (pbk.)
   [1. Brothers and sisters—Fiction. 2. Babies—Fiction.] I. Lamb, Stacey, ill. II.
Title. III. Series.

PZ7. F8475 Si 2002
[E]—dc21   2001047204

© 2002 by Betsy Franco
Illustrations © 2002 by Stacey Lamb
All rights reserved. Published simultaneously in Canada.
Printed in the United States of America.
1 2 3 4 5 6 7 8 9 10 R 11 10 09 08 07 06 05 04 03 02

Sally is so silly!

I smile.

Sally smiles.

I snap.

Sally smiles.

I skip.

Sally smiles.

I sing.

Sally smiles.

Sally smiles.

21

I smile!

Word List (10 words)

I	sing	snap
is	skip	so
Sally	smile	
silly	smiles	

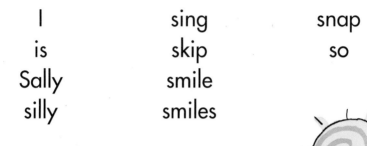

About the Author

Betsy Franco lives in Palo Alto, California, where she has written more than forty books for children—picture books, poetry, and nonfiction. Betsy is the only female in her family, which includes her husband, Douglas, her three sons, James, Thomas, and David, and Lincoln the cat. She starts writing in the wee hours of the morning when everyone but Lincoln is asleep.

About the Illustrator

Stacey Lamb "became" an artist in the fourth grade, when she discovered that she could draw the Peanuts character Snoopy, and has been drawing ever since! She grew up in Illinois  and went to the University of Kansas. Today, she lives out in the country in Lawrence, Kansas, with her husband, Brent, two children, Emily and Scott, and one dog, eight cats, one bunny, and one pet mouse.